P9-DEK-697

CONTENTS

EVERY DAY
WITH
JESUS®

~

Devotional Collection

THE
CHARACTER
OF GOD

Two Full Months of Daily Readings by
SELWYN HUGHES

**BROADMAN
& HOLMAN
PUBLISHERS**

Nashville, Tennessee

EVERY DAY WITH JESUS®—THE CHARACTER OF GOD
Copyright © 2004 by Selwyn Hughes
All rights reserved

Broadman & Holman Publishers
Nashville, Tennessee
ISBN 0-8054-2737-6

Unless otherwise indicated, all Scriptures are taken from the Holy Bible,
New International Version ® copyright © 1973, 1978, 1984 by International Bible Society.
Used by permission of Zondervan Publishing House. All rights reserved.

Other translations are identified as follows:

NKJV
New King James Version. Copyright © 1979, 1980, 1982 by Thomas Nelson, Inc.
Used by permission. All rights reserved.

TLB
The Living Bible, copyright © Tyndale House Publishers,
Wheaton, Illinois, 1971, used by permission.

Amplified
The Amplified Bible, Old Testament copyright © 1962, 1964 by
Zondervan Publishing House, used by permission, and the New Testament
© The Lockman Foundation 1954, 1958, 1987, used by permission.

KJV
The King James Version

Dewey Decimal Classification: 242.64
Subject Heading: DEVOTIONAL LITERATURE

Printed in the United States of America
2 3 4 07 06 05 04

INTRODUCTION

Too few people embark on this most noble quest: to mine and discover the riches of God's character. Even among those who begin, the appeal of more practical topics often pulls them away in midstream. God's love, power, and glory—though strong enough to speak the heavens into place—are not always attractive enough to hold the modern attention span.

Oh, how much we need to know of God! How many more hours we should be spending in worship and wonder rather than dealing with the small coinage of our own needs and concerns. For when given permission to dominate our thoughts, our personal matters become impossible to satisfy. We could speak of them all day long and never tire of their finest details. Yet in even the tiniest fingertip of God's character rests enough hope and security to consume all our problems and personal issues in His provision. He is all! And He is enough!

So you have made a wise choice to spend this time dealing day-by-day with God's attributes. Even so, we can but mention a few of His many characteristics, and at best only glance at even those we've chosen to study. It is a lifetime's refreshing work to know God more fully, and we will need eternity itself to even scratch the surface. Yet we begin again, knowing that He will show us all we are ready to receive.

THE PRIMARY FOCUS

"In the beginning God." (1:1)

❧

We focus on what is without doubt the most noble and loftiest of themes: the nature and character of God. I have noticed that Christians, generally speaking, seem to be preoccupied with knowing more about themselves rather than knowing more about God. Ask any Christian bookshop manager: "What are the best-selling books?" Not those that unfold for us the nature of God, but those that direct us toward such things as how to get a better self-image, how to manage money, how to find inner healing, how to get more excitement out of life, and so on. Not that these subjects are unimportant, but they are explored in a self-absorbed way that gives the idea that the most important thing in life is knowing ourselves better. It isn't. The most important thing in life is knowing *God* better.

John Lancaster, a minister in Cardiff, South Wales, in an article entitled "Where on Earth Is God?" asks the question: "Given a choice between attending a seminar, say, on the 'Glory of God in Isaiah' and one on 'The Christian and Sex,' to which would you go?" He makes the point also that although the

6

church often answers the questions that people are asking, the real problem may be that people are not asking the right questions. In today's church we are far too man-centered and not God-centered.

It is not by accident, I believe, that the Bible opens with the thunderous acclaim: "In the beginning God." I tell you with all the conviction of which I am capable: if God is not our primary focus, then everything else will soon get out of focus.

PRAYER

O Father, from this day help me determine to make You my primary focus. And give me the grace and strength to maintain it, through all the vicissitudes and uncertainties of the days ahead. In Jesus' name I pray. Amen.

FURTHER STUDY

John 1:1-5; Col. 1:15-20; Heb. 12:2; Rev. 1:8
What did the Lord declare to John the revelator?
What did the apostle John declare?

A LOST ART

"Who has known the mind of the Lord?
Or who has been his counselor?" (11:34)

~

A subject which is of great interest to many today is anthro-
pology: the study of man. Although this subject is of great
importance, for a Christian there is something far more important: the study of God. The great preacher C. H. Spurgeon said:
"The highest science, the loftiest speculation, the mightiest
philosophy that can ever engage the attention of a child of God
is the name, the nature, the person, the work, the doings, and
the existence of the great God whom he calls his Father."

The contemplation of God seems to be a lost art today. We
appear to be more concerned about subjects such as church
growth, the end times, signs, wonders, and miracles. I am not
suggesting these issues are unimportant, but they must not be
allowed to replace the supremely important matter of the constant, earnest, and continued investigation of the great subject
of the Deity. The more we know of God, the more effective
will be our lives here on earth. Those who have given themselves
to the study of God tell us that it humbles the mind, expands

8

the soul, and consoles the heart.

It humbles the mind. When our minds grapple with other subjects, we feel a degree of self-content and come away thinking: "Behold, I am wise." But when our minds engage with thoughts of God, we discover that there is no plumb-line that can sound His depth, and we come away thinking: "Behold, I know nothing." In an age which stresses the supremacy of the human ego, it is no bad thing to learn that there is something far greater.

PRAYER

Gracious and loving heavenly Father, teach me how to focus on You and contemplate You so that all vanity and pride dies within me, and I go on my way no longer caught up with how wise I am but how wonderful You are. In Jesus' name. Amen.

FURTHER STUDY

Isa. 40:18-26; Job 11:7-9
What probing question does Isaiah ask?
What conclusion had Zophar come to?

QUIET CONTEMPLATION

"You make me glad by your deeds, O LORD." (92:4)

~

We said that the contemplation of God humbles the mind, expands the soul, and consoles the heart.

How does it *expand the soul?* "The soul," says one theologian, "is at home only when it is in God." He meant, of course, that as the soul was made for God, it can only function effectively when indwelt by God. Contemplation of God is like breath to the soul; it inflates it and causes it to be fully actualized. "My body and my whole physiology functions better when God is in it," said a doctor to me some years ago. I replied: "And so it is also with the soul, dear doctor, so it is also with the soul."

The third benefit of contemplating God is that it *consoles the heart.* But how? It does so by focusing the heart's attention on the greatness and goodness of the Eternal and also on His tender mercies and compassion. The more we know of God, the more we realize that when He permits us to pass through deep and dark waters, it is not because He is powerless to deliver us, but because a beneficent and eternal purpose is being worked out in that process. And what is more, we discover that God is not interested merely in working out His purposes in us, but in imparting to us a richer sense of His presence. In God there is a balm for every wound, a comfort for every sorrow, and healing for every heartache.

All kinds of nostrums are on offer in today's church to help the hurting (some of them more secular than sacred), but I know of nothing that calms the swelling billows of sorrow and grief as does the quiet contemplation of the Godhead.

PRAYER

My Father and my God, forgive me if in times of trial and distress I look for comfort in the wrong places. You and You alone are able to meet my soul's deepest needs. Help me to see this not merely as an opinion but as a conviction. In Jesus' name. Amen.

FURTHER STUDY

Psa. 145:1-21; Deut. 32:1-4; 1 Chron. 29:10-13
How did David express the feelings of his soul?
How did Moses put it?

"ECCENTRIC" CHRISTIANS

FOR READING AND MEDITATION—
ISAIAH 40:21-31

"He sits enthroned above the circle of the earth,
and its people are like grasshoppers." (40:22)

∾

The man-centered focus that is creeping into today's church must be resisted at all costs. Such matters as disciplining children, dealing with marital problems, and establishing proper priorities should be addressed also, but we must be careful that "market forces" do not mold our theology.

It could be argued that our problems are so acute because we are deficient in our knowledge of God. The context in which we think and feel is so limited that it is no wonder our souls feel stifled and claustrophobic. One preacher describes our condition in this way: "We are like Peter trying to walk on the water but becoming so engrossed in the winds and the waves that we lose sight of the all-sufficient Christ who is right there beside us. The immediate environment has blotted out the sense of the eternal."

This is why I have chosen today's reading from the magnificent book of Isaiah. The prophet does what a doctor would do upon visiting a patient with a minor sickness and finding the windows shut fast and the room lacking in oxygen. He would throw open the windows and invite the patient to inhale the purer air. "Take a deep breath of the oxygen of the Spirit," Isaiah is saying in effect. "See how great and powerful God is. Set your problems in the context of His omnipotence."

We become like the thing we focus on. If we center on man rather than God, then we ought not be surprised if we finish up off center—eccentric.

PRAYER

O God, save me from being an off-center Christian and thus an eccentric Christian—the true meaning of that term. May my primary focus be always on You. Grant it, dear Lord. In Jesus' name I pray. Amen.

FURTHER STUDY

2 Cor. 4:13-18; Heb. 3:1; 12:2; Psa. 141:8
What was Paul's focus?
What is the exhortation of the writer of Hebrews?

STIRRED, BUT NOT SHAKEN

FOR READING AND MEDITATION—
PSALM 16:1-11

*"Because he is at my right hand,
I shall not be shaken." (16:8)*

~

Whenever I have the opportunity to address Christian counselors, I try to urge them to put the glory of God before their client's well-being. A good deal of "Christian counseling" today follows the client-centered approach, where the person is all-important. Thus more attention is paid to how the person has been hurt by others than how he or she may be hurting God by being unwilling to trust Him. This is a very sensitive issue, and I tell counselors in training that it must never be brought up until other issues have been explored and understood. But ultimately, however, this is the issue we must all face, whether we are in counseling or not.

Ask yourself this question now: Do I allow myself to be more overwhelmed by the wrong which people have done to me than the wrong I might have done (and may still be doing) to God by my unwillingness to trust Him? Putting the glory of God before our well-being does not go down well with some modern-day Christians brought up in the "me" generation. It means that we have to break away from the idea that life revolves around our desires, our ambitions, our self-image, our personal comfort, our hurts, and our problems, but instead around the glory and the will of God. When we learn to apply the great text before us today to our lives, we will find, as did the psalmist, that when we set the Lord always before us, then no matter what happens, we will be stirred but not shaken.

PRAYER

Father, thank You for reminding me that I cannot avoid my soul being "stirred" by life's problems, but when I have set You ever before me, then I can avoid being "shaken." Drive this truth deep into my being this very day. In Jesus' name. Amen.

FURTHER STUDY

1 Sam. 4:1-22; Ex. 33:12-18; Psa. 29:1-2
Is there a parallel between this account and today's church?
What was Moses' request?

GOD MARGINALIZED

*"But let him who boasts boast about this:
that he understands and knows me." (9:24)*

❧

A minister speaking at a recent conference of a well-known denomination said: "The reason why there is so much depletion of spiritual energy in people nowadays is due to the rush of modern-day life." But is this really true? If it is, then it puts the blame for our condition *outside of* us rather than *inside* us— the place (in my opinion) where the fault really lies. No, the real reason for the spiritual dullness in so many lives is that we have lost our sense of priority.

One of my favorite poets is Wordsworth, and I simply love the lines that go thus:

The world is too much with us; late and soon

Getting and spending we lay waste our powers;

Little we see in Nature that is ours;

We have given our hearts away.

"The world is too much with us!" Therein lies our problem. Other things, other issues, other problems, other priorities have been allowed to press in upon us, and the consequence of all this is that God has become marginalized. If we were to pay as much attention to the things that pertain to God as we do to the things that pertain to the world, then the spiritual health of the church (generally speaking) would not be such a cause for concern. Through the prophet Jeremiah, God speaks to us and shows us that His greatest desire is that we should come to know Him. When we lose God, we lose touch with reality, for reality, as one great Christian put it, is Jesus' other Name.

PRAYER

O God, forgive me that so often my desires are at cross-purposes with Your desires. My desire is to know more about me; Your desire is for me to know more about You. Help me bring my desires in line with Your desires. In Jesus' name. Amen.

FURTHER STUDY

Jer. 2:1–13; 17:13: Isa. 53:6
What two sins had Israel committed?
At what broken cisterns does the church drink?

"Nutty" Is the Word

*"Your love is like the morning mist,
like the early dew that disappears."* (6:4)

⁓

A danger that we must acquaint ourselves with as we discuss the need to contemplate God more deeply is that of becoming more interested in godliness than in God Himself. Theologian Jim Packer puts the point effectively when he says that "moving in evangelical circles as I do, I am often troubled by what I find. While my fellow believers are constantly seeking to advance in godliness, they show little direct interest in God Himself. When they study Scripture, only the principles of personal godliness get their attention; their heavenly Father does not. It is as if they should concentrate on the ethics of marriage and fail to spend time with their spouse!" He goes on to say: "There is something narcissistic, and, to tell the truth, nutty in being more concerned with godliness than about God."

I think "nutty" is the right word.

I knew a man who went to every seminar he could find on the subject of marriage, and whenever he came upon a new idea or a deep insight, he would reflect for hours on its wonder and profundity. The only trouble was he never got past the reflecting stage, and while he indulged himself in new and profound ideas, his wife was left languishing at home.

How sad that a man can take more interest in the principles that undergird his marriage than in the partner whom he has pledged to love, honor, and cherish. Let's be watchful that we don't care more for the principles of godliness than the God we are called to praise and please every day of our lives.

PRAYER

Gracious and loving heavenly Father, forgive me, I pray,
if I have been caught up more in the mechanics of my faith
than in the dynamics of it. May nothing ever become more
important to me than my relationship with You. Amen.

FURTHER STUDY

2 Tim. 3:1-5; 2 Chron. 25:1-2; Isa. 29:13
What is one of the signs of the last days?
What is said of Amaziah?

SEEING THE INVISIBLE

FOR READING AND MEDITATION—
HEBREWS 11:17-28

"He persevered because he saw him who is invisible." (11:27)

∽

What is it that prompts some people to take more interest in the principles of godliness than in God Himself? I think one reason could be that we are more comfortable dealing in the realm of the visible than the invisible. We prefer to work with things we can touch, handle, and apply so that we feel an immediate impact rather than to launch out into the unseen and to simply trust.

I often saw people come up against this problem in the days when much of my time was spent in personal counselling. I would bring people to a place where they could accept that the roots of their problem lay in a deficient relationship with God. However, when a movement of simple basic trust toward Him was called for, terror would appear for a moment in their eyes and they would say: "Give me some steps I can take to deal with my problem, some principles I can follow that will act as a ladder on which I can climb out of this pit."

We all find it easier to do than to be; we prefer a plan to follow rather than a Person to trust. What our carnal nature hates to be faced with is the challenge of throwing ourselves in utter dependency on a God who is invisible and intangible. Yet this is what a relationship with God entails. The thing that marks Moses out as outstanding in the chapter before us today is not his works but his faith. He persevered because he saw Him who is invisible. It is possible to see the invisible, but it is possible only to the eye of faith.

PRAYER

*My Father and my God, help me recognize this terrible
tendency in myself to be more comfortable with working than
trusting. Let Your Word reach deep into my heart today.
Teach me how to be. In Jesus' name I pray. Amen.*

FURTHER STUDY

Rom. 1:16-23; Heb. 11:1-2; 1 Tim. 1:17
Why are men without excuse?
What is the essence of faith?

BALANCED CHRISTIANITY

"After beginning with the Spirit, are you now trying to attain your goal by human effort?" (3:3)

❧

The Christian church has always struggled to get the balance right between faith and works. Romans is the great book on "faith," while James is the great book on "works." I know some Christians who never read the book of James, taking sides with Martin Luther who called it a "book of straw." Martin Luther may have been right about many things, but he was wrong when he referred to the Epistle of James in this way. We need to study both Romans and James if we want to be properly balanced Christians.

The difficulty with faith and works is this: we come into the Christian life by depending on Jesus' innocent sufferings on Calvary as sufficient ground for our acceptance with God, and then when we learn the principles of Christian living, we turn from dependency on Christ to dependency on them. This was the great problem in the Galatian churches, and it is still a problem here in the church of the current century. Bringing forth the fruit of repentance by good works is terribly important, but we are not to depend on works for our salvation.

We tend to focus more on works than faith because it is something visible and tangible. We can see what we are doing and assess it or measure it. Faith is different. It requires of us a degree of helplessness (something the carnal nature detests), but if we are to know God better and avoid falling into the trap of pursuing godliness more keenly than pursuing God, then faith must be seen as the primary virtue.

PRAYER

O Father, help me get this right. I am saved to good works, but I am not saved by good works. Prevent me from falling into the trap of being more preoccupied with Your principles than with You Yourself. In Jesus' name. Amen.

FURTHER STUDY

Eph. 2:1-9; Gal. 2:16: Rom. 9:32
What did Paul remind the Ephesians?
What did he emphasize to the Galatians?

MEETING THE PERSON

*"I want to know Christ and the power
of his resurrection." (3:10)*

~

It must not be assumed that the study of Scripture and the contemplation of the principles which God has built into His Word are unimportant. They most certainly are. But let us be on our guard that we do not fall into the trap of contemplating the principles which God has built into the universe more than God Himself.

I have often seen students of Scripture fall into this trap when, in reading their Bible, the only things that get their attention are the principles that relate to godliness. They underline them in their Bible, mark alongside them other Scriptural references, and think that by doing this they are growing spiritually. The problem, however, is that only the principles of daily personal godliness capture their interest; their heavenly Father does not.

Imagine treating a love letter that way: identifying and underlining the principles, reflecting on the profundity of some of the insights, marveling at the clarity of the language and yet missing the main purpose of the letter—romantic passion and love. Yet this is the way some people approach the Bible. Our aim in studying the nature and character of God must be to know God better (not merely know His Word better), and we must seek to enlarge our acquaintance not simply with the characteristics of His nature, but with the living God whose characteristics they are.

PRAYER

O God, help me never to approach the Bible content to know only the written Word. Give me a passion that never remains satisfied until, through the written Word, I discover more of the living Word. In Jesus' name. Amen.

~

FURTHER STUDY

Rev. 2:1-7; 2 Cor. 5:14
What was the church in Ephesus commended for?
Why was this insufficient?

GOD'S SELF-REVELATION

"But those who trust in idols . . .
will be turned back in utter shame." (42:17)

❧

Most of what we know about God is from His self-revelation in the Scriptures. We know something about Him as we look out through the lattice of nature, but because the world of nature has been affected by the Fall, we cannot expect to find a clear revelation of Him there.

Scripture, however, is different. The Bible (I believe) has been supernaturally protected from the effects and influences of sin, and in its pages we have a clear revelation of who God is and what He is like. This is why all human ideas about God, His will, and His work—both traditional and contemporary—must be ruthlessly brought in line with what Scripture says.

Those who think they can get a clear picture of God apart from Scripture are misguided and deceived. A young Christian once said to me: "I don't need to read the Bible to know God; I simply sit and meditate on Him, and He reveals Himself to me." He thought he could know God in this way, but he was mistaken. When we try to know God or understand Him

26

through the medium of our own conceptions, then our conceptions are the medium.

The Bible is God's revelation of Himself, and unless our thoughts are guided and constantly corrected by God's thoughts, we will soon go off at tangents. We need to remember that idolatry—which means forming unbiblical notions of God and thus worshipping unrealities—is the sin that is most frequently denounced in Scripture.

PRAYER

O God, help me understand more than ever that it is the entrance of Your Word that gives light, and the neglecting of Your Word that gives darkness. May I take Your light as my light, and thus walk through life with a sure and steady tread. Amen.

~

FURTHER STUDY

Ex. 20:1-7; Deut. 11:16; 1 John 5:21
What were the children of Israel to be careful about?
What was John's admonition to the church?

THE GREAT CREATOR

FOR READING AND MEDITATION—
ISAIAH 42:1-9

*"He who created the heavens and stretched them out,
who spread out the earth . . ." (42:5)*

～

The Bible never argues that there is a God; everywhere it assumes and asserts the fact. Majestically the opening verse of Scripture says: "In the beginning God . . ." Its paramount concern is not to persuade us *that* God is, but to tell us *who* God is and what He does. This is why the first thing we see Him do in the Scriptures is to act creatively, to show His might and omnipotence.

I love the story about a group of researchers who set out to discover what really happened when the earth was created. They spent months gathering information and feeding data into a computer. Finally they hit the printout key and waited. Soon a message appeared with these words: "See Genesis 1:1."

Many think the only reference to God's creative act is the one which appears in the first two chapters of Genesis, but this truth is woven inextricably into the very texture of both the Old and New Testaments. One example of this is found in our text for today. We cannot have a right conception of God or contemplate Him correctly unless we think of Him as being all-powerful. He who cannot do what He wills and pleases cannot be God. As God has a will to do good, so He has the necessary power to execute that will. Who can look upward to the mid-night sky, behold its wonders, and not exclaim: "Of what were these mighty orbs formed?" A great and powerful God brought them into being simply by saying: "Let them be." This kind of God can have my heart anytime.

PRAYER

Father, I sense that the more enlightened my understanding, the more my soul responds to that enlightenment with thanksgiving, adoration, and praise. Enlighten me still more, dear Father. In Jesus' name I pray. Amen.

≈

FURTHER STUDY

Acts 14:8-15; Neh. 9:5-6; Psa. 102:25; Heb. 11:3
What did Paul and Barnabas declare?
How do we understand that God formed the universe?

"NOT FROM ME!"

FOR READING AND MEDITATION—
PSALM 33:1-22

*"By the word of the LORD were the heavens made,
their starry host by the breath of his mouth." (33:6)*

～

Many modern astronomers probing into outer space with their gigantic telescopes favor two theories as to the origin of the universe. One is the so-called Big Bang Theory, according to which "the cosmos started with a titanic explosion, and as a consequence has been expanding ever since." The other is the Continuous Creation Theory which maintains that "the universe is self-creating and is constantly making itself out of nothing and falling back into nothingness again."

What many scientists are not prepared to admit is that the ultimate energy behind the universe is a not a Big Bang, but a Big Being—an intelligent Being of indescribable majesty and power who is able to do whatever He chooses. And because what He chooses is always good, He can be trusted to have the best interest of His creation at heart.

When Joseph Haydn, the famous Austrian composer, had finished his great oratorio *The Creation*, he is said to have cried: "Not from me! Not from me! From above it has all come!" Our text for today reminds us that by God's Word were the heavens made and by His breath the stars were formed.

I once heard my father describe the creation in this way: "It was no harder for God to create a world than it is for my son to blow soap bubbles into the air out of his clay pipe." I often go back to that lovely image. I find that when contemplating this awesome, mighty, all-powerful God, my soul instinctively cries: "How great Thou art." I hope yours does too!

PRAYER

Yes Father, as I contemplate Your majesty and Your power, my soul cries out: "How great Thou art." It can do nothing else, for contemplation of You inevitably leads to adoration of You. Amen.

∼

FURTHER STUDY

Matt. 19:16-26; 1 Chron. 29:12; Psa. 62:11; Isa. 43:12-13
What did Jesus declare?
What did God declare?

Sustained and Secure

*"These all look to you to give them their food
at the proper time." (104:27)*

❦

No creature has the power to preserve itself. "Can papyrus grow tall where there is no marsh?" asked Job (Job 8:11). Both man and beast would perish if there were no food, and there would be no food if the earth were not refreshed with fruitful showers. As one preacher put it: "We came from God's hand and we remain in His hand."

Think of the marvel of life in the womb. How an infant can live for so many months in such a cramped environment—and without breathing—is unaccountable except for the power of God in preservation. It was divine preservation Daniel was thinking of when he said to the godless Belshazzar: "You did not honor the God who holds in his hand your life and all your ways" (Dan. 5:23). Everywhere in the Scriptures God is presented not only as the Creator of the world but as its Sustainer and Preserver also. God has not wound up the universe like a clock and then separated Himself from it; rather, He is active in sustaining it, and were He to remove Himself from it, it would cease to exist.

The writer to the Hebrews reminds us that He is "upholding all things by the word of his power" (1:3, KJV). If the maker of some artifact were to die, his death would make no difference to it. It would continue to exist just as it did before. Not so with God and His world, however. If God were to die the universe would fall to pieces. But don't worry—God cannot die. The universe is quite secure.

PRAYER

O God, when I consider how You are my Sustainer and my Preserver, my heart is humbled before You. You cannot die, and because I am linked to You, I cannot die. I know my body will die, but my soul is Yours forever. Thank You, dear Father. Amen.

FURTHER STUDY

Isa. 46:1-13; Psa. 18:35; 147:6
What did the Lord underline to the children of Israel?
What did the psalmist testify?

THIS GOD IS YOUR GOD

FOR READING AND MEDITATION—
EZEKIEL 22:1-16

*"Will your courage endure or your hands
be strong in the day I deal with you?"* (22:14)

❧

God is powerful in judgment. When He smites, none can resist Him. The flood of Noah's day is one such example, when the entire race—with the exception of eight people—was swept away (Gen. 6:1-9:18). When a shower of fire and brimstone fell from heaven on Sodom and Gomorrah, all the cities of the plain were destroyed (Gen. 19:1-29). Pharaoh and his hosts found themselves impotent when God blew upon them at the Red Sea (Ex. 14:1-31).

What does the contemplation of God's power do for us?

First, it causes us to tremble before Him. The trouble with many modern men and women is that they do not tremble before God. To treat with impudence the One who can crush us more easily than we can a tiny ant is, as someone put it, "a suicidal policy." "Kiss the Son," said the psalmist, "lest he be angry and you be destroyed . . . for his wrath can flare up in a moment" (Psa. 2:12).

Second, contemplating God's great power causes us to adore Him.

Who can consider the might of this awesome God without wanting to worship Him? The rebellious heart will resist this, but the heart cleansed by the blood of Christ will bow in homage and say: "Who is like you—majestic in holiness, awesome in glory, working wonders?" (Ex. 15:11). No prayer is too hard for Him to answer, no need too great for Him to supply, no predicament too great for Him to solve. Lay hold on this great and gripping truth: this God is your God.

PRAYER

O Father, I see that contemplation of You tilts my soul
in Your direction. I realize that without You I am nothing.
May I tremble before You until my trembling turns to
adoration and ever-increasing trust. Amen.

~

FURTHER STUDY

Psa. 114:1-8; 1 Chron. 16:30-31; Isa. 66:1-3
What can the presence of the Lord do?
Who does the Lord esteem?

THE GOD WHO SPEAKS

*"So are my ways higher than your ways
and my thoughts than your thoughts." (55:9)*

❧

After seeing in Genesis I that God is all-powerful, the next thing we observe about God is that He is personal. But what does it mean to be a person? What predicates personality?

The best definition of personality I know is the one given to me by the tutor who taught me theology: "To be a person, we have to be able to think, to reason, to feel, to judge, to choose, and to communicate in words that constitute a language." Richard Swinburne, a theologian, observes that people use language not only to communicate and for private thought, but to argue, to raise a consideration, to object to another. Unlike animals which show evidence only of wanting food and drink, people can want *not* to want something—like a fasting man, for example, wanting not to want food.

Now with that in mind—that one of the constituents of personality is the ability to think and speak—read the first chapter of Genesis once again. Notice how many times the words appear: "God said." Count them. God is portrayed to us

as a speaking God. And because speech is one of the constituent parts of personality, this proves to us that the Deity is
a personal Being. We are not long into Genesis before we are
brought face-to-face with the fact that there is more to God
than mere power; the Almighty is a Person. This means, among
other things, that the Almighty cannot be studied from a "safe"
distance. Because He is a Person, He is someone who wants and
waits to be known.

PRAYER

*Loving heavenly Father, how thankful I am that You made me like
Yourself—to know and be known. May my strongest desire be to
know You, not merely to know myself. For it is only when I
know You that I can most truly know myself. Amen.*

~

FURTHER STUDY

Gen. 1:1-31; Job 33:13-14; 1 Kings 19:12; Ezek. 43:2
How many times does it say "God said"? //
How did Ezekiel describe God's voice?

"PLENTY OF TIME FOR YOU"

*"How precious to me are your thoughts, O God!
How vast is the sum of them!" (139:17)*

～

The constituent parts of personality are predicted of God on almost every page of the Bible. "I will raise up for myself a faithful priest, who will do according to what is in my heart and mind," said the Lord to Eli in I Samuel 2:35. This shows (if it needs showing) that God has a mind with which He thinks.

God has emotions also—another aspect of personality. Some modern-day theologians claim that God is unable to feel, but clearly this is not supported by Scripture. God can be angry (Psa. 2:12), jealous (Zech. 1:14-15), merciful (Psa. 78:38), and joyful (Deut. 30:9). These are just a few of the emotions which Scripture talks about, but there are many more. Again, God chooses and decides. "And it repented the LORD that he had made man on the earth. . . . And the LORD said, I will destroy man whom I have created." (Gen. 6:6-7, KJV).

While the majority of people believe in some kind of God, many view Him as being so great that He cannot possibly take a personal interest in such insignificant creatures as ourselves.

Dr. Henry Norris Russell, one of the great astronomers of this century and a Christian, once gave a talk on the vastness of the universe. Afterwards, someone asked him this question: "How is it possible for such a great and infinite God to have time for me?" This was his reply: "An infinite God can dispatch the affairs of this universe in the twinkling of an eye, thus giving Him plenty of time for you."

PRAYER

O Father, help me in the midst of every trial and difficulty to drop my anchor in this reassuring and encouraging revelation: no matter what my problem, You always have plenty of time to give to me. I am so deeply, deeply thankful. Amen.

FURTHER STUDY

Heb. 4:12-16; Psa. 2:12; Zech. 1:14-15;
Psa. 78:38; Deut. 30:9

Can you think of other Scriptures showing God's emotions?
What is God able to do through Christ?

JITTERY THEOLOGIANS

*"But God said . . . 'You fool! This very night
your life will be demanded from you.'"* *(12:20)*

❧

Why is it that so many in our day and age are attracted to
the notion of a God who is impersonal? New Age theories
seem to be infiltrating all parts of society in almost every country of the world.

I think there is a very subtle reason why men and women prefer to think of God as a power rather than as a person. If God
is merely a power, or a formless life-force flowing through the
universe, He can make no demands. One is not challenged to
relate to an energy in the same way that one is challenged to
relate to a person. When we believe God is a Person, the next
question we have to face is: "How do I relate to Him?" It is the
idea of meeting a personal God which causes men and women
to tremble.

But deep down in every human heart, placed there by the
Almighty, is a conviction that a personal God exists. We have
all been made in His image, and His stamp is upon us whether
we like it or not. In reality there are very few atheists; most

people believe in some kind of God.

Someone has described an atheist as "a theologian with the jitters." A good way of dealing with those jitters is to expunge from the heart the idea that God may be personal and that one might be accountable to Him. Better a life-force or a celestial energy—a power that can be tapped—rather than a Person one might some day have to meet. How foolish it all is—settling for short-term comfort but facing eternal loss.

PRAYER

Father, I am saddened when I realize how so many want to run from You when their best interests lie in running to You. Draw many to You this very day, dear Lord. In Jesus' name. Amen.

❧

FURTHER STUDY

Gen. 1:26-30; 5:1; 1 Cor. 11:7; James 3:9; Eccl. 3:11
What are the implications of being created in God's image?
What has God set within us?

THE GOD WHO IS THERE

"The fool says in his heart, 'There is no God.'" (14:1)

～

The idea of a living, personal God gives men and women the jitters. They sense deep within that they are accountable to Him, but they don't know just what to do about it.

C. S. Lewis put it like this: "The Pantheist's God does nothing, demands nothing. He is there if you wish for Him, like a book on a shelf. He will not pursue you. There is no danger that at any time heaven and earth should feel awe at His glance. But Christ the Creator King is there. And His intervening presence is terribly startling to discover." Lewis goes on to compare the shock of discovering that there is a living, personal God in the universe to sitting alone in the dark and sensing someone breathing beside you. "It is always shocking," he says, "to meet life where we thought we were alone."

Listen to this paragraph by Lewis which I quote in full, as it puts the truth in a way that cannot be equaled: "There comes a moment when the children who have been playing at burglars hush suddenly; was that a real footstep in the hall? There comes a moment when people who have been dabbling in religion suddenly draw back. Supposing we really found Him! We never meant it to come to that! Worse still, supposing He has found us? So it is a sort of Rubicon. One goes across, or not. But if one does, there is no manner of security against miracles. One may be in for anything."

No one need worry about getting any shocks when they steadfastly resist believing in a personal God. No shocks, but no salvation either.

PRAYER

Gracious God, how can I ever sufficiently thank You for bringing me to Yourself? The thought of a God who is alive, taking a personal interest in me, is more than I can comprehend. Yet I believe it. With all my heart. Thank you dear Father. Amen.

~

FURTHER STUDY

Psa. 10:1-4; 36:1-4; 1 John 2:22
What is at the heart of the atheist?
How does John describe those who deny Christ?

THE FATHER GOD

"When you pray, say: 'Father'" (11:2)

~

Samuel Shoemaker, the American Episcopalian preacher who was instrumental in forming Alcoholics Anonymous, pointed out that the whole principle of prayer depends on what kind of Being the Creator is. Listen to this statement made to a group of recovering alcoholics: "If He created the universe and gave everything a primeval push, and then retired beyond where we cannot get in contact with Him, prayer is a vain effort. But if He be a personal God as Christians believe He is, then He will have a concern for the people He made and will want to involve Himself with them in all their affairs." We are not alone in this universe; a personal God stands behind all things, waiting, longing that we might enter into a relationship with Him.

We said that one of the reasons why people desire an impersonal God is because this kind of God is easier to live with than one who is personal like themselves. It's rather nice to carry inside our hearts a subjective idea of a God of beauty, truth, and goodness. That kind of God demands nothing of us. Better still a formless life-force surging through all of us, a vast power we can tap and use to our advantage. This kind of God is extremely easy to live with.

But a living God who approaches us at infinite speed—the Hunter, the King, the Lover, the Husband—this is quite another matter. Yet whether we believe it or not, this is the kind of God He is.

PRAYER

How thankful I am that You are not just a supernatural energy or a life-force, but a personal Being whom I can address as Father. Your personality engages with my personality, and we are one. In this my joy knows no bounds. Amen.

~

FURTHER STUDY

Gen. 3:1-8; Ex. 33:14-17; Isa. 43:2
How did God present Himself as a personal Being?
What did He promise Moses?

ON THIS TRUTH WE STAND

"Jesus . . . saw . . . the Spirit descending. . . . And a voice came from heaven: 'You are my Son.'" (1:10-11)

~

Those who accept Scripture's teaching concerning God must be prepared to say that He is not only personal, but that He is a *plurality* of Persons—a Trinity. The doctrine of the Trinity, that God is one yet three separate Persons, is not easy to understand, but it is clear in Scripture. The term "Trinity" nowhere appears in the Bible (it was first used by Tertullian around A.D. 210), but its roots are deeply embedded in the Word of God. It is mainly a revelation of the New Testament, but there are glimpses of the truth to be seen in the Old Testament also.

"Let us make man in our image" (Gen. 1:26). To whom was God speaking? Some say the angels, but nowhere in Scripture are angels seen as being involved in the act of creation or as being on the same level as God. Read Colossians 1:16 and it will become clear to whom God was speaking.

Other examples of the Trinity being mentioned in the Old Testament include these: "Man has now become like one of us" (Gen. 3:22). And in Isaiah 6:8 God says: "Whom shall I send?

And who will go for us?"

"Go to the Jordan," wrote Augustine, "and you find the Trinity. There at the baptism of Jesus, the three Persons in the Godhead are simultaneously in evidence. The Father is heard speaking directly from heaven, the Son is seen being immersed in the river, and John the Baptist beholds the Spirit descending upon the Christ." Three in One and One in Three. On this truth we must stand, though we may not fully understand.

PRAYER

Blessed Trinity, Three in One and One in Three,
my spirit joins with Your Spirit this day to worship You in
spirit and in truth. Though sometimes darkness to my intellect,
Your truth is nevertheless sunshine to my heart. Amen.

~

FURTHER STUDY

Matt. 28:16-20; John 14:26-27; 15:26-27
How were the disciples to baptize new converts?
How did Jesus confirm the truth of the Trinity?

THE BAPTISMAL FORMULA

FOR READING AND MEDITATION—
MATTHEW 28:1-20

*"Baptizing ... in the name of the Father
and of the Son and of the Holy Spirit." (28:19)*

~

We ended the previous reading with the words of Augustine, which reminded us that if we want to see the Trinity in action, all we have to do is to go to the River Jordan. It was Augustine who pointed out also that the Trinity can be seen in the verse that is before us today, which we call "the baptismal formula." Note that we are bidden to baptize in the name (not "names") of the Father, Son, and Holy Spirit, indicating their essential unity and oneness.

I know there are many in the Christian church who do not accept the doctrine of the Trinity, and this makes me very sad. I just wish they would look at the matter again, for I have found it to be one of the most satisfying of doctrines, as it meets the greatest needs of my soul. George Matheson spoke for me and millions of other Christians when he said:

Some seek a Father in the heavens above,
Some ask a human figure to adore,
Some crave a Spirit vast as life and love,

Within thy mansions we have all and more.

Alfred Tennyson, a man with an incisive mind who saw deep into the creation, put it like this: "Though nothing is such a distress of soul to me as to hear the divinity of Christ assailed, yet I feel I must never lose the unity of the Godhead, the three persons being like three candles giving together one light." Note his words: "I must never lose the unity of the Godhead."

I would simply add: neither must we. Neither must we.

PRAYER

Father, Son, and Holy Spirit, I freely confess that my mind finds it difficult to comprehend how You can be Three in One, and One in Three. Yet this is the teaching of Scripture. So I believe; help Thou mine unbelief. In Jesus' name. Amen.

FURTHER STUDY

2 Cor. 13:1-14; 1 Thess. 5:19-24
How does Paul affirm the truth of the Trinity?
How does he illustrate it?

THREE GREAT ERRORS

"I urge you . . . by our Lord Jesus Christ and by the love of the Spirit . . . by praying to God . . ." (15:30)

~

"God is One, yet God is Three. How can such a strange thing be?" These are the lines of a ditty that supposedly was sung by troops on the march in World War I. Theologians down the ages have tried to illuminate this doctrine for us, but it is an issue that will never be fully clarified until we arrive in heaven (I Cor. 13:12). Basically the doctrine of the Trinity is: God is One but with three distinct centers of consciousness. Around this truth a number of errors have been propounded.

The first was the teaching that there are three gods. The Jehovah's Witnesses accuse present-day Christians of believing this, and say that we conceive of God as a body with three heads. That might be true of ancient heresy, but it is not true of classic Trinitarianism. *The second heresy taught that God is unipersonal* and the other two Persons in the Trinity are simply manifestations of the one God. *The third main error denied the equality of the divine Persons* and regarded them as being of different rank.

The historic church formulated the Athanasian Creed, which

states that we worship one God in Trinity and Trinity in unity. What we must see, however, is that no words can fully explain the truth of the Trinity. "The creed is a safety net to keep us from falling into error," says one preacher, "rather than a verbal net in which to trap the truth." We use the term "Trinity" expecting not so much that in that one word the truth may be spoken, but that it may not be left unspoken.

PRAYER

Father, I see that life often presents me with facts which seem irreconcilable at one stage of knowledge, though better understood at another. Perhaps one day this great mystery of the Trinity may be cleared up. Meanwhile I simply worship and adore. Amen.

≈

FURTHER STUDY

1 Pet. 1:1-6; 1 Tim. 2:5
How did Peter distinguish the members of the Trinity?
What did Paul confirm to Timothy?

LOGICALLY NECESSARY

"Give thanks to the God of gods.
His love endures forever." (136:2)

～

The Trinity is implicit in the whole Bible from the beginning, though it might not be evident to someone unfamiliar with the Book who started reading at Genesis until they had reached the books of the New Testament.

Ian Macpherson, in his book *The Faith Once Delivered*, says that when the island now known as Trinidad was discovered by Columbus, he thought at first it was three islands, as all he could see were three hills silhouetted against the sky. When he got closer, however, he found that what he had seen was not three islands at all but just one island. From a distance it looked like three, but close up it was only one. Hence he named the island "Trinidad"—Spanish for "Trinity."

That is the kind of experience you get when reading the Bible. At first it seems to be talking about three Gods, but as you go deeper into the Scriptures you discover there are not three Gods but one—one God in three Persons.

It must be noted, though, that it is not only in isolated texts that one encounters the doctrine of the Trinity. The very concept of God's love presupposes plurality in the Godhead. Love, to be love, must have an object. Self-love is love's opposite. Since God (as we shall see more closely later) is eternal love, He must have had objects of eternal affection. The objects of His affection were the Son and the Spirit. The doctrine of the Trinity, therefore, is not only theologically but logically necessary to an understanding of the nature of the Deity.

PRAYER

Father, help me understand that a being fully comprehended could not be God. In Your unfathomable depths all my thoughts are drowned. Symbolically I remove my shoes, for I sense I stand on holy ground. Amen.

FURTHER STUDY

Eph. 4:1-6; Deut. 4:35; Psa. 83:18; 1 Cor. 8:4
What did Paul confirm to the Ephesians and Corinthians?
What was the psalmist's conviction?

THE GREAT TRIUNE GOD

FOR READING AND MEDITATION—
JOHN 20:19-30

*"Thomas said to him,
'My Lord and my God!'"* (20:28)

～

Dr. W. E. Sangster tells the story of following three children out of church. One remarked to the others: "I can't understand all this 'Three in One and One in Three' business."

"I can't either," said another child, "but I think of it like this: my mother is Mummy to me, she is Mabel to Daddy, and Mrs. Douglas to lots of other people."

Is that the answer? Is it just a question of names? Are we right in finding the doctrine of the Trinity in the text of Matthew 28:19, where the word "name" is singular, but three names are given—Father, Son and Holy Spirit?

No, that is just part of it; there is much more to it than that. God, we know, is one God. But there stepped into the world someone who claimed also to be God. His name was Jesus. He forgave sins, claimed to have existence before Abraham, and accepted worship as His right. Worship, remember, is for God alone. After Jesus was resurrected and returned to heaven, He sent back the Holy Spirit, who was also seen as God (2 Cor.

13:14). He—the Holy Spirit—came into the disciples and brought with Him the resources of the Godhead, breaking the sin in their nature, pleading in prayer, and exalting the Savior.

Thus we see God is One but also Three in One: God above us, God among us, God within us. The Father in majesty, the Son in suffering, the Spirit in striving. This is the central mystery of our most holy faith. Together, and with all our hearts, let us adore the great triune God.

PRAYER

Father, Son, and Holy Spirit, though I cannot comprehend Your essential oneness and unity, I can worship You nevertheless. This I do now, in humble adoration. Glory, honor, and power be unto Your name forever and ever. Amen.

FURTHER STUDY

John 1:1-14; 8:58; 10:30; 17:5
How did John describe Jesus?
What did Jesus declare of Himself?

A WATERSHED TRUTH

*"The grace of the Lord Jesus Christ . . . the love of God
. . . the fellowship of the Holy Spirit . . ." (13:14)*

❧

That great Christian, Francis Schaeffer, said that he would
have remained an agnostic if it weren't for the doctrine of the
Trinity. It was this, he claimed, that gave him the answer—the
only answer—to the theme of unity and diversity.

The question I have been asked most often about the Trinity
is this: Why did not God make clear the truth of the Trinity in
the Old Testament, rather than leaving it as something to be
deduced in the New Testament? I usually answer like this:
Before God could entrust His people with the knowledge of
His essential Threeness, He had to lay deep in their minds a
piercing conviction of His Oneness. The Bible begins in
monotheism (belief in one God), but soon after the Fall comes
polytheism (belief in many gods). Which god is the real God?
Not until belief in one God was laid deep in the consciousness
of the Jewish nation was God ready to reveal more clearly to
mankind the sublime truth of the Trinity.

Dr. George Smeaton says: "The biblical idea of the Trinity

is the heart of the unique message of Christianity. To explain this mystery is not our province. Ours is simply to conserve the mystery." Those who call themselves Christians yet reject the doctrine of the Trinity will soon latch onto some other error. It is a strange thing, but I have observed it as a fact of the Christian life that when this truth is modified or pushed aside, it is as if the door is opened to the inrush of all kinds of absurd ideas, bizarre theories, and half-truths.

PRAYER

Father, help me hold fast to this sublime truth, and enable me to see that though something is above reason, it is not necessarily against reason. Blessed Trinity—Father, Son, and Holy Spirit—I worship You. Amen.

FURTHER STUDY

John 14:8-21; 17:22
How did Jesus depict the Trinity?
What did Jesus confirm?

THE HIGH-WATER MARK

"God is love." (4:16)

～

We turn now to consider another aspect of God's nature and character—love. There are at least three things that are told us in Scripture concerning the nature of God.

First, "God is spirit" *(John 4:24),* which means He has no visible substance.

Second, "God is light" *(1 John 1:5),* which means no darkness can dwell in Him. In Scripture darkness stands for sin, death, and so on.

Third, "God is love," which means that the energy which flows out from His being is that of infinite, eternal beneficence.

When John wrote the words "God is love," it was no slick statement, since it was the first time in history that the phrase had been used in that way. People had believed God was love and had speculated about His benevolence, but now the categorical statement was laid down for all to behold. These words, in my judgment, are the high-water mark of divine revelation; nothing more needs to be said, for nothing greater can be said.

I often create a mental picture for myself of the angels peering over the battlements of heaven as John wrote these words. And then, when they had been written down, I imagine them breaking into rapturous applause and saying to each other: "They've got it. They've got it! At last they see that God is love." A sigh of deep satisfaction and great joy would have filled the portals of heaven in the knowledge that the greatest truth about God was now finally made crystal clear. The implied was now inscribed.

PRAYER

Father, I am so thankful that You have demonstrated categorically that the greatest thing about You is love. My heart gladly rests upon that glorious fact. I look forward to exploring it forever.

~

FURTHER STUDY

Jer. 31:1-4; John 3:16; Rom. 5:8
What did the Lord appear and say?
How did He demonstrate this?

AMAZING LOVE!

"The LORD did not . . . choose you because you were . . . numerous. . . . It was because the LORD loved you." (7:7-8)

～

When the Bible says God is love, it is saying more than the fact that God loves, or that God is loving, or even that God is lovely; it is saying that love is the power behind everything He does. Love is not merely one of His attributes but His whole nature. God is not only the Author of loving acts; He is love in the very core of His being. Our thoughts of God's love must be built on God's revelation about Himself in the Scriptures, not by projecting our own ideas about love on to Him. Let's focus, therefore, on what the Bible has to say about the God who is love.

First, God's love is uninfluenced. By this I mean that nothing in us can give rise to it and nothing in us can extinguish it. It is "love for nothing," as someone once put it.

The love which we humans have for one another is drawn out of us by something in the object of our love. But God's love is not like that; His love is free, spontaneous, and uncaused. The passage before us today makes clear that there is no reason behind the love of God for His people. If you look for a reason, you just won't find one. He loves because . . . He loves.

No man or woman can ever explain why God loves us. To explain it would require that He loves us for something outside of Himself. And as we have seen, He loves us for ourselves alone. His love has its beginning not in us but in Himself. He is love's source, as well as its river.

PRAYER

O God, what security this gives me to know that Your love for me will never be diminished and never be taken away. Help me reflect on this and draw from it the inspiration I need to walk tall and strong through every day. In Jesus' name. Amen.

FURTHER STUDY

Eph. 2:1-10; 1 John 3:1
How does Paul describe God's reason for saving us?
How does John put it?

WHAT A TRANQUILIZER!

FOR READING AND MEDITATION—
JEREMIAH 31:1-12

"I have loved you with an everlasting love." (31:3)

~

"How little real love there is for God," says theologian Arthur W. Pink. He suggests that the low level of spirituality in today's church is caused by our hearts being so little occupied with thoughts of the divine love. "The better we are acquainted with His love—its character, its fullness, its blessedness," he says, "the more will our hearts be drawn out in love to Him."

We focus now on the fact that *God's love is eternal.*

God being eternal, it follows that His love also is eternal. This means that God loved us before earth and heaven were called into existence, that He has set His heart upon us from all eternity. This is the truth set forth in Ephesians 1:4-5, where we are told that we were chosen in Christ before the foundation of the world. What a tranquilizer this is for our hearts! If God's love for us had no beginning, then it has no ending either. It is from "everlasting to everlasting."

Another thing we need to know about the love of God is that *it is a holy love.* This means that His love is not regulated by whim or caprice or sentiment, but by principle. Just as His grace reigns not at the *expense* of righteousness but "through" it (Rom. 5:21), so His love never conflicts with His holiness. This is why John says that God is "light" before he says God is "love." And this is why, too, the Almighty never lets us get away with anything. He loves us too much for that. His love is pure, holy, and unmixed with maudlin sentimentality. God will not wink at sin, not even in His own people.

PRAYER

O Father, the more I learn about Your love, the more my heart is set on fire. Increase my understanding, for I see that the more I comprehend how much I am loved, the more secure I am in that love. Amen.

FURTHER STUDY

Rom. 8:18-39; 1 Pet. 1:17-21
What was Paul convinced of?
How does Peter portray the eternal perspective?

LOVE CREATING LOVE

"We love because he first loved us." (4:19)

~

Although the love of God is clearly laid out in the Old Testament, why did humankind have to wait so long to have the message spelled out in such clear terms as John uses: "God is love"? People could not see this sufficiently clearly until they had looked into the face of Jesus. In the life of Jesus is the clearest revelation that God is love.

So few of us open ourselves to the love of God. We have more fear of Him than we have love for Him. There is, of course, a godly fear (or reverence), but that is not what I mean. If we fail to comprehend how much we are loved by God, then there will be no energy to turn the machinery of our lives in the way they were meant to turn.

Whenever I doubted the love of God as a young Christian, I was told I should go to Calvary. I never quite understood what that meant until one day I complained to God that He could not really love me; if He did, He wouldn't let such things happen as were befalling me. He gave me no answer but showed me the cross. And as I saw His Son dying there for me, the scales fell from my eyes and I found love for Him flowing out of His love for me. I discovered what the verse at the top of the previous page meant: "We love because he first loved us."

Love for God is not the fruit of labor but the response of our hearts to being loved. It is not something we manufacture; it is something we receive.

PRAYER

O God my Father, save me from believing that my problem is "I don't love You enough," when the real problem is "I don't know how much I am loved by You." Let the scales fall from my eyes right now and let me see—really see. In Jesus' name. Amen.

❧

FURTHER STUDY

John 19:16-30; Eph. 2:15-16; Col. 1:19-22
What is the result of the cross?
Spend some moments in prayer contemplating the cross.

THE CROSS'S MAGNETISM

"But I, when I am lifted up from the earth, will draw all men to myself." (12:32)

~

The love for God that burns in our hearts must never be seen as the fruit of our labor, as if it is something we manufacture. Seeing the love of God for us, our own hearts respond with love. We give love for love. We cannot help it. Let's be done with the idea that love for God is something we work at. It issues forth in good works, of course, but it begins in contemplation of how much we are loved.

I often tell my students that they cannot love until they have been loved. By this I mean that love is a response. Our souls must receive love before we can give out love. Those who did not receive much love from their parents complain at this stage: "I can't love God, because my soul was never properly prepared to love; my parents didn't love me."

This is a problem, I agree, but it must never be seen as an insoluble problem. No one who stands at Calvary and sees God dying for them on that tree can ever argue that because they were not loved by their parents, they cannot now receive God's love. If they really believe that, then they are saying that God's love is balked by the adverse influence of human conditioning.

God's love will only flow into us if we let it and if we really want it. To desire it is like the touch of the hand on a spring blind: the blind is released and the sunlight flows in. Just to want His love is enough; He will do the rest.

PRAYER

O God, forgive me if I have used excuses to barricade my heart against Your love. I gaze once more on Calvary and open my heart to allow its mighty magnetism to draw my soul toward You in a way it has never been drawn before.

~

FURTHER STUDY

2 Thess. 3:1-5; Jude 21; Eph. 3:17-19
What was Paul's desire for the Thessalonians?
What was Paul's prayer for the Ephesians?

QUALITY PAR EXCELLENCE

FOR READING AND MEDITATION—
ISAIAH 6:1-13

"Holy, holy, holy is the LORD Almighty." (6:3)

❧

The next aspect of God's nature and character we examine is that of His holiness. Even the most casual reader of the Scriptures cannot help but notice that God is portrayed in the Bible as uniquely and awesomely holy. In fact, there are more references to the holiness of God in Scripture than to any other aspect of His character. This ought to give us some indication of how important it is.

But what do we mean when we say God is "holy"? There are three thoughts underlying the word "holy."

First, the idea of separation, being withdrawn or apart.

Second, brightness or brilliance.

Third, moral majesty, purity, or cleanliness. It is interesting that those who came into direct contact with the Almighty in the Old Testament were inevitably overwhelmed by His moral majesty.

Isaiah went into the temple to pray at a time when his people were in grave difficulties. Uzziah, the king who had ruled for half a century, was dying and Assyria, a terrible and evil force, stood threateningly to the north. Whatever answer Isaiah thought he would get as he opened up his heart to God, it was not the one he received. He was given instead a vision of a holy God that shook him to the core of his being.

Why should this be? I think it was because the concept of God's holiness is the main lesson in His school, the divine prerequisite for admission to the inner heart of God, the most important qualification for learning from the Lord.

PRAYER

Father, I must search my heart this day and ask myself: Do I know what it is to serve a holy God? Have I ever received a vision of the moral majesty and purity of the Divine? Deepen my understanding of all this I pray. In Jesus' name. Amen.

∼

FURTHER STUDY

Ex. 15:1-11; Psa. 99:9
What question did Moses pose?
What did the psalmist affirm?

TOWARD PERFECTION

FOR READING AND MEDITATION—
DEUTERONOMY 10:12-22

*"What does the LORD your God ask of you
but to fear the LORD your God?" (10:12)*

∼

The first thing God called Israel to do—when He announced that they were to be His special people and to live the way He wanted them to live—was to fear Him. Loving Him, serving Him, and keeping His laws were of great importance, of course, but the very first things God asked of them were reverence and fear.

How does all this relate to the love of God? When thinking about God, it is wise to see love and holiness as intertwined; not to do so can sometimes lead to serious error.

Many in today's church present the love of God in such a way that it has given rise to the saying "God loves me as I am." The idea in many minds is: "God loves me as I am, and whether I go on from here or whether I stay the same, it makes no difference to His love for me." This is entirely true, but it is not the entire truth. Because God is love, He loves us as we are, but because He is *holy* love, He loves us too much to let us stay as we are. Yes, we can be secure in the fact that God loves us just the way we are, but the holy love of God calls us to move ever closer to Him. It cries out: "Be holy as I am holy."

Error is truth out of balance. We need to rejoice in the fact that we are loved because of who we are and not for what we do, but we must see also that God's love is a holy love and thus will inevitably prod us toward perfection.

PRAYER

O Father, help me keep these two things in balance—both your love and your holiness. Don't let the security I feel as I rest in Your love turn to smugness and complacency. Show me that though I am "accepted in the Beloved," that does not mean You don't want me to come closer. Amen.

∿

FURTHER STUDY

1 Sam. 6:1-21; Rev. 15:4

What question did the men of Beth Shemesh ask?

What truth was revealed to John in the song of the Lamb?

THE CONSUMING FIRE

FOR READING AND MEDITATION—
HEBREWS 12:14-29

"Our 'God is a consuming fire.'" (12:29)

~

George MacDonald writes: "Nothing is inexorable but love, for love loves unto purity. Love has ever in view the absolute loveliness of that which it beholds. Where loveliness is incomplete, and love cannot love its fill of loving, it spends itself to make more lovely, that it may love more; it strives for perfection even that itself may be perfected—not in itself but in the object. Therefore all that is not beautiful in the beloved, all that comes between and is not of love's kind, must be destroyed. Our God is a consuming fire."

Powerful words.

The nature of God is so terribly pure that it destroys everything that is not as pure as fire. God desires us to worship Him in "the beauty of holiness" (Ps. 29:2, KJV). This means that He wants the purity in us to match the purity in Him. We cannot arrive at this purity by self-effort, of course, but the more we draw nigh to Him, the more the fire of His purity will burn out the dross within us.

"It is not the fire that will burn us up if we do not worship," said George MacDonald, "but the fire will burn us up *until* we worship." And the fire will go on burning within us after everything that is foreign to it has been consumed, no longer with pain and a sense of something unwanted being consumed, but as the highest consciousness of life.

God is a consuming fire. He always was, and always will be— world without end.

PRAYER

O God, I long with all my heart that my worship might be all You want it to be. May Your consuming fire burn out all the dross within me until everything that is foreign to Your nature is part of me no more. In Jesus' name I ask it. Amen.

FURTHER STUDY

Psa. 97:1-5; Isa. 66:15; 1 Cor. 3:12-14
What does the psalmist say about fire?
What will the fire do?

THE FEAR OF GOD

FOR READING AND MEDITATION—
PROVERBS 8:1-21

"To fear the LORD is to hate evil." (8:13)

~

We are taught over and over again in Scripture that because God is uniquely and awesomely holy—pure, separated, and shining in His moral majesty—we are to draw near to Him with godly reverence and fear. The fear of the Lord, as we know, is the beginning of wisdom. Contemplation of His character, particularly His holiness, will lead to a reverential fear that prepares the soul (as it did for Isaiah) for more profitable service and activity.

But what does it mean to "fear" God? There are times in the Bible when we are told to fear, and times when we are told *not* to fear. There is a fear that helps and a fear that hinders. How do we know the difference?

The fear that helps is the fear that expresses itself in reverence, veneration, awe, a sense of grandeur and majesty of God. The fear that hinders is described for us in 2 Timothy 1:7: "For God did not give us a spirit of timidity, but a spirit of power, of love and of self-discipline."

The Greek word *deilia*, which is translated "timidity" in this verse, comes from a root that means "wretched, sorry, miserable" and implies someone lacking in courage. God is not to blame for attitudes of cowardice or timidity; they come from within our own hearts. Timid people are frightened people, and if you want to explore this thought still further, ask yourself: What kinds of things frighten me that are not related to the fear of God? If we fear them more than we fear God, then we are being ruled by the wrong kind of fear.

PRAYER

O God, I bring to You all my unhealthy fears and lay them at Your feet. Help me develop such a reverential fear for You that all other fears are quickly swallowed up. In Jesus' name. Amen.

∾

FURTHER STUDY

Deut. 10:1-12; Josh. 24:14; Eccl. 12:13
What did the Lord require of Israel?
What did Joshua admonish Israel to do?

THE POWER OF HOLINESS

FOR READING AND MEDITATION—
PSALM 99:1-9

*"Exalt the LORD our God and worship
at his footstool; he is holy." (99:5)*

❧

No one can know the true grace of God," said the great Bible teacher A. W. Tozer, "who has not first known the fear of God." He continued: "Always there was about any manifestation of God something that dismayed the onlookers, that daunted and overawed them. . . . I do not believe any lasting good can come from religious activities that are not rooted in this fear. Until we have been gripped by that nameless terror which results when an unholy creature is suddenly confronted by the One who is holiest of all, we are not likely to be affected by the doctrine of love and grace."

There was a time when the nature and character of God was a constant theme in Christian pulpits, but not any more. Generally speaking, today's preachers (and writers) tend to give people what they want rather than what they need. This is why we must stop every time we come across a reference to God's character in our Bibles and pause to consider it. No one has done anything mighty for God without a new vision of God's holiness. Ezekiel tells us of the "rims" in his vision that were "high and awesome" (Ezek. 1:18), and Jacob, rising from his sleep, said: "How awesome is this place!" (Gen. 28:17).

We will be of little use to God unless we know how to tremble before Him, for otherwise our own ideas and feelings of self-sufficiency will soon take over. Have we lost the sense of awe when we come into God's presence which seemed to characterize the saints of the past? I am afraid we have.

PRAYER

O God, I am afraid as I draw near to You, but I draw near because I am afraid. Nothing or no one can dissolve the fears that hinder me but You. Draw me closer, for in You and You alone lie both my salvation and sanctification. Amen.

≈

FURTHER STUDY

Ex. 3:1-5; Josh. 5:15; Psa. 33:8; 89:7
What was Moses' and Joshua's experience?
What did the psalmist admonish?

OUR TRUSTWORTHY GOD

FOR READING AND MEDITATION—
DEUTERONOMY 7:7-20

*"He is the faithful God, keeping his covenant
of love to a thousand generations." (7:9)*

❧

<u>God is utterly trustworthy in all He says and does</u>, and this
is the rock-bottom reality on which everything in the universe
depends. In an age when so much unfaithfulness abounds, how
good it is to realize that we have One who will never let us
down, never have to apologize for failing us, and never go back
on His Word.

Am I speaking to someone who has just discovered unfaithfulness in a marriage partner, or experienced the break-up of a
relationship because a person you trusted did not keep their
word? It's a sad moment when we get a revelation of the incon-
sistency of the human heart. But we need to look into our own
hearts also, for none of us can claim complete immunity to the
sin of unfaithfulness. We may not have broken a contract or
violated the marriage covenant, but we have been unfaithful to
Christ in other ways—to the light and privileges which God
has entrusted to us, perhaps.

How refreshing it is, then, to read today's text and focus our gaze on the One who is faithful at all times and in all things. We may let *Him* down, but He will never let *us* down.

A chorus I learned as a young Christian comes back to me when I am tempted to doubt the faithfulness of God:

> *He cannot fail for He is God,*
> *He cannot fail, He pledged His Word,*
> *He cannot fail, He'll see you through,*
> *He cannot fail, He'll answer you.*

PRAYER

Gracious and loving God, what inspiration it brings to my soul to realize that of all the things You can do, the one thing You can't do is fail. May the reality of this be the pavement on which I tread this day and every day. In Jesus' name. Amen.

FURTHER STUDY

1 Kings 8:54-61; Psa. 89:1-8
What did Solomon testify?
What did the psalmist promise to do?

GREAT FAITHFULNESS

*"Your love, O LORD, reaches to the heavens,
your faithfulness to the skies." (36:5)*

~

How wonderful it is, in an age where unfaithfulness abounds, to focus our gaze on those Scriptures that point to the trustworthiness of our God. The one before us today is quite wonderful, but consider also these:

"O LORD God Almighty, who is like you? You are mighty, O Lord, and your faithfulness surrounds you" (Psa. 89:8).

"Righteousness will be his belt and faithfulness the sash round his waist" (Isa. 11:5).

"If we are faithless, he will remain faithful, for he cannot disown himself" (2 Tim. 2:13).

Can't you just feel the energy flowing from these Scriptures, buttressing your confidence in God? For God to be unfaithful would be to act contrary to His nature, and if He ever was (we are only speculating because He could never do so) then He would cease to be God. Focus again with me on the text at the top of the page. We are told God's faithfulness extends to the skies. This is the psalmist's picturesque way of expressing the fact that far above all finite comprehension is the unchanging faithfulness of God. Everything about God is vast and incomparable, including His faithfulness. He never forgets a thing, never makes a mistake, never fails to keep a promise, never falters over a decision, never retracts a statement He has made, and has never breached a contract. Every declaration He has made, every promise He has given, every covenant He has struck is vouchsafed by His faithful character.

PRAYER

O God, how great Thou art. Great in power, great in majesty, great in love, great in mercy—great in so many things. But above all You are great in faithfulness. How I rejoice in that. Amen.

FURTHER STUDY

1 Cor. 1:1-9; Heb. 6:18; 1 Pet. 4:19
What did Paul assure the Corinthians?
What is it impossible for God to do?

THE NEED TO KNOW

FOR READING AND MEDITATION—
HEBREWS 10:19-31

*"Let us hold unswervingly to the hope we profess,
for he who promised is faithful."* (10:23)

~

The Bible is a veritable mine of information on the fact of
God's faithfulness. More than 4,000 years ago He said: "As
long as the earth endures, seedtime and harvest, cold and heat,
summer and winter, day and night will never cease" (Gen.
8:22). Every year furnishes us with fresh evidence that He has
not gone back on His Word.

In Genesis 15:13-14, God declared to Abraham: "Know for
certain that your descendants will be strangers in a country not
their own, and they will be enslaved and ill-treated four hundred years. But . . . afterwards they will come out with great
possessions." Did that happen? Exodus 12:41 says: "At the end
of the 430 years, to the very day, all the LORD's divisions left
Egypt."

The prophet Isaiah predicted that a virgin would conceive
and bear a son whose name would be Immanuel (Isa. 7:14).
Centuries later the prediction came to pass. In Galatians 4:4 we
read: "But when the time had fully come, God sent his Son,

born of a woman."

I wish I had the space to take you through the pages of Scripture and show you how faithful God has been to His Word. But you have a Bible for yourself; study it. Read it to know God. This is the basis of our confidence in Him. And this is why the Bible fairly bulges with this great and gripping truth. The more of God's truth we pack into our souls, the better equipped we are for the road that lies ahead.

PRAYER

Gracious and loving Father, the more I learn about Your nature and character, the more I want to know. Just these glimpses I am getting set my soul on fire to know You more intimately. Take me deeper, dear Lord. In Jesus' name. Amen.

FURTHER STUDY

Mal. 3:7; Psa. 103:17; 102:27; James 1:1-17

What did the Lord declare to Israel?

How did James put it?

STANDING ON PROMISES

*"He has given us his very great
and precious promises." (1:4)*

❧

It is one thing to accept the faithfulness of God as a clear biblical truth; it is quite another to act upon it. God has given us many great and precious promises, as our text for today puts it, but do we actually count on them being fulfilled?

We have to be careful that we do not hold God to promises He has *not* given. I have seen a good deal of heartache suffered by Christians because someone encouraged them to take a statement from the Word of God, turn it into a "promise," and urged them to believe for it to come to pass. Then when nothing happened, they became deeply discouraged.

One woman told me that many years ago she had taken the words found in Acts 16:31—"Believe in the Lord Jesus, and you will be saved—you and your household"—and claimed them as a promise. When her husband and son died unrepentant, she was devastated. I pointed out to her that even God cannot save those who don't want to be saved, and that the promise given by Paul and Silas was for the Philippian jailer, not anyone else.

There are hundreds of promises that God has given in His Word that we can claim without equivocation. Someone who has counted all God's promises in the Bible numbers them as being over 3,000. That ought to be enough to keep you going if you lived to be a hundred. Be careful, however, that it is a *general* promise you are banking on, not a *specific* one.

PRAYER

Father, I have Your promise that You will guide me into all truth, so my trust is in You that You will give me the wisdom to discern between a promise which is general and one that is specific. In Jesus' name. Amen.

~

FURTHER STUDY

Heb. 1:1-12; 13:8; 2 Cor. 4:18
Why is Jesus so dependable?
Where do we fix our eyes?

HE CAN'T FORGET!

Jesus answered, "The work of God is this:
to believe in the one he has sent." (6:29)

～

In the passage before us today, our Lord is asked: "What must we do to do the works God requires?" (v. 28). His answer was entirely different from that which you would receive if you posed the question to adherents of different religious systems today. A Buddhist would answer: "We must follow the eight-fold path of Buddhism." A Muslim would answer: "We must fast and pray and make a trip to Mecca." Some followers of the Christian way might answer "We must engage in regular Bible study, prayer, tithing, and Christian fellowship." But the answer Jesus gave was this: "The work of God is this: to believe . . .'"

George Watson, a devotional writer, said: "To trust the Origin of our existence is the fundamental grace of life. There is one virtue [in God] that stands out forever more conspicuously than friendship, or love, or knowledge, or wisdom. It is fidelity. *God's fidelity is in Him what trust is in us*" (emphasis mine). Understanding that God is utterly trustworthy will deliver us from such incapacitating emotions as worry, anxiety, and fear. To be overwhelmed by the concerns of this life reflects poorly upon the faithfulness of God.

An old saint who was dying became concerned that he couldn't remember any of God's promises. His pastor said: "Do you think God will forget any of them?" A smile came over the face of the dying Christian as he exclaimed joyfully: "No, no, He won't." This, too, is our confidence. He *won't* forget, because being God, He *can't* forget.

PRAYER

O God my Father, if fidelity in You is what trust is in us,
then help us come to a place where our trust matches Your fidelity.
We confess we are not there yet, but we long to arrive.
Help us, dear Father. In Jesus' name. Amen.

~

FURTHER STUDY

2 Tim. 2:1-13; Heb. 2:17; 10:23
What did Paul assure Timothy?
Why was Jesus made like His brothers?

No Blemish in God

FOR READING AND MEDITATION—
DEUTERONOMY 32:36-47

"I will take vengeance on my adversaries and repay those who hate me." (32:41)

∿

We turn now to focus on an aspect of God's character which for some reason many see as a blotch or blemish in the divine nature. I refer to the matter of God's wrath. Though the subject may be missing from many modern-day pulpits, it is not missing from the Bible. If you look up in a Bible concordance all the texts that refer to the wrath, anger, or the severity of God, you will find that there are more references to these than there are to His love, graciousness, or tenderness. A proper study of God can never be complete unless consideration is given to the fact that God is not only a God of love but a God of wrath and anger also.

I remember in the early days of my Christian experience that whenever I heard any reference to the wrath of God, I would feel a deep resentment arise within me, and instead of regarding this aspect of God's nature with delight, I looked upon it with disdain. Later, however, when I came to understand it and saw it in its proper light—as something to rejoice in rather than to be resented—I found my love for God and my awe of God swell to new proportions.

Arthur W. Pink describes the wrath of God as the "eternal detestation of all unrighteousness . . . the displeasure and indignation of divine equity against evil . . . the holiness of God stirred into activity against sin." Never view the wrath of God as a moral blemish or a blotch on His character. It would be a blemish if wrath were absent from Him.

PRAYER

Father, I would face all reality—even those aspects that do not fit into my preconceived ideas. Help me not to balk at the idea that You are a God of wrath as well as a God of wonder. In Jesus' name I pray. Amen.

∼

FURTHER STUDY

2 Kings 22:1-13; Psa. 90:11
Why did God's anger burn?
What did the psalmist say about God's wrath?

GOD'S GREAT INTOLERANCE

FOR READING AND MEDITATION—
ISAIAH 5:18-25

*"They have rejected the law of the LORD Almighty. . . .
Therefore the LORD's anger burns." (5:24-25)*

∾

Wrath is not a defect in the divine character; rather, it would be a defect if wrath were absent from Him. Those who see God's wrath as petulance or retaliation, inflicting punishment just for the sake of it or in return for some injury received, do not really understand it. Divine wrath is not vindictiveness; it is divine perfection, issuing forth from God because it is right.

Human beings tend to make God in our own image. He made us in *His* image, but we want to return the compliment, and it is there that so often we go wrong. Instead of reasoning from the divine down to the human, recognizing that sin has marred the divine image within us, we reason from our fallen condition and project our own feelings and ideas onto God.

Thus, when thinking of the wrath of God, we tend to look at what happens in our own hearts when we get angry, and we imagine God to be the same. But divine anger must never be confused with human anger. Most of what goes on in our hearts whenever we are angry is a mixture of unpredictable petulance, retaliation, hostility, and self-concern. God's anger is always predictable, always steadfast, and always set against sin. We must never forget that God's nature is uncompromisingly set against sin. We may tolerate it; He never.

Sin has been defined as "God's one great intolerance," and for that we ought to be eternally grateful. As His children we ought to rejoice that He will not tolerate anything that is harmful to us.

PRAYER

O Father, what a change comes over me when I realize that Your wrath is not so much directed at persons but at the sin that demeans and destroys them. You are not against me for my sin, but for me against my sin. I am deeply, deeply grateful. Amen.

~

FURTHER STUDY

Psa. 5:1-6; 11:5; Hab. 1:12-13; Zech. 8:16-17
How did the psalmist express God's great intolerance?
What does the Lord hate?

RIGHTEOUS INDIGNATION

FOR READING AND MEDITATION—
ROMANS 1:8-25

"The wrath of God is being revealed . . . against all the godlessness and wickedness of men." (1:18)

∼

For many of us, "wrath" conjures up the idea of being out of control, an outburst of "seeing red," a sense of wounded pride or just downright petulance. But it is quite wrong to take these ideas or feelings and impose them on God. God's wrath is never out of control, never capricious, never self-indulgent, never irritable, and never ignoble. These may be indicative of human anger but never of the divine. God is angry only when anger is called for.

Even among men and women, there is such a thing as righteous indignation, though (in my opinion) it is more rare than we think.

I used to believe the difference between righteous indignation and carnal hostility was this: when someone was angry with *me*, that was carnal hostility; when I was angry with *someone else*, that was righteous indignation! I have "grown out" of that opinion now, I hasten to add.

All God's indignation is righteous. It is grief at what is happening to others, not a grudge because of what is happening to Him. Would a God who took as much pleasure in evil as He did in good be a God we could love? Would a God who did not react adversely to evil be morally perfect? Of course not. It is precisely this adverse reaction to evil that the Bible has in mind when it talks about God's wrath. God cannot treat good and evil alike. He can *look over* it—look over it to the cross where it can be forgiven—but He cannot *overlook* it.

PRAYER

O God, the more I see the reason behind Your wrath and the more I consider the purity of its motive, the more praise and adoration I want to give. What a great and wonderful God You are. And how glad I am You looked over my sin. Amen.

~

FURTHER STUDY

Isa. 13:1-22; Psa. 78:40-55; Isa. 30:27
How does the psalmist describe God's wrath?
How did Isaiah depict God's anger toward Babylon?

THE UNYIELDING JUDGE

*"Settle matters quickly with your adversary
who is taking you to court." (5:25)*

∽

"God's wrath," said George MacDonald, "is always judicial. It is always the wrath of the Judge administering justice. Cruelty is always immoral, but true justice—never." Those who experience the fullness of God's wrath get precisely what they deserve. This may sound hard, but it is true.

There is great wisdom in the words of our Lord in the passage before us today. Settle matters with an adversary, He says, before he drags you to court. Do at once what you must one day do anyway. There may be no escape from payment, but why not escape at least from the prison sentence that will enforce it?

The point our Lord is making is that we ought not to drive justice to extremities. God requires righteousness of us, does He not? It is utterly useless to think, then, that we can escape the eternal law. So yield yourself rather than be compelled.

To those whose hearts are true, the idea of judgment is right; to those whose hearts are untrue, the idea of judgment is wrong. Many people live under the illusion that perhaps it might be possible to find a way of escaping all that is required of us in this world. But there is no escape. A way to avoid the demands of righteousness, apart from the righteousness which God accounts to us at the cross, would not be moral. When a man or woman accepts the payment God has made for them in Christ, the whole wealth of heaven is theirs; their debt is cleared. Those who deny that debt or who, acknowledging it, do nothing to avail themselves of the payment made for them on Calvary, face an unyielding Judge and an everlasting prison.

PRAYER

O Father, how serious and solemn is all this, but yet how true. Sin must ultimately be punished. I am so grateful that in Christ my debt has been paid, and availing myself of Your offer I am eternally free. Blessed be Your name forever. Amen.

~

FURTHER STUDY

Zeph. 3:1-5; Psa. 103:6; John 5:30; Rom. 2:2
What does God do morning by morning?
What is God's judgment based on?

HEAVEN OR HELL

"In hell, where he was in torment, he looked up and saw Abraham far away." (16:23)

❧

The final state of those who die without availing themselves of God's freely offered forgiveness is eternal banishment from God's presence. The Bible calls this "hell." "There is no heaven with a little hell in it," said George MacDonald, meaning that the God who is passionately *for* righteousness and implacably *against* sin must ensure that the two are finally separated.

However, hell is always something that people choose for themselves. It is a state for which men and women opt. Before hell is experienced as eternal, it is always experienced as something temporary in the sense that, as men and women retreat from the light God shines into their hearts to lead them to Himself, they experience in a small way what they will experience in full when they are banished into "outer darkness" (Matt. 25:30, KJV). Dorothy Sayers described hell as "the enjoyment of one's own way forever." God says to those who die impenitent: "You preferred your own way to mine; you shall have it—forever." In the last analysis, all that God does in consigning people to hell is to allow them to face the full consequences of the choice they have made. God is resolute in punishing sin, and hell is the final consequence of this.

I know most of my readers are Christians, but I know also some are not. Those of you reading these lines who have never surrendered your lives to Christ, I urge you to surrender your hearts to Him today. Christ has died to save you from hell. Pray this prayer with me now.

PRAYER

Father God, I come to You now through Your Son, the Lord Jesus Christ. I repent of my sin, ask Your forgiveness, and receive You into my life as Savior and Lord. Thank You, dear Lord. Amen.

FURTHER STUDY

Matt. 5:27-30; 18:7-9; 25:34-43
How did Jesus illustrate the importance of avoiding hell?
How can we be sure of avoiding hell?

LOVE WITH A "STOOP"

FOR READING AND MEDITATION—
HEBREWS 4:1-16

*"Let us then approach the throne
of grace with confidence." (4:16)*

❧

Grace is more than a synonym for love; it is a characteristic of the Deity which is quite close to love (and mercy) but yet deserves to be seen as different and distinctive. I heard an old Welsh preacher say: "Grace is a word with a 'stoop' in it; love reaches out on the same level, but grace always has to stoop to pick one up." It was probably this same thought that an anonymous writer had in mind when he said: "Grace is love at its loveliest, falling on the unlovable and making it lovely."

But it is to the great Puritan preacher Thomas Goodwin we must turn for the best clarification of the difference between love and grace: "Grace is more than mercy and love. It superadds to them. It denotes not simply love but love of a sovereign, transcendentally superior One that may do what He will, that may freely choose whether He will love or no. There may be love between equals, and an inferior may love a superior, but love in a Superior—and so superior that He may do what He will—in such a One love is called grace. Grace is attributed to princes; they are said to be 'gracious' to their subjects, whereas subjects cannot be gracious to princes."

Grace then is God's kindness bestowed upon the undeserving; benevolence handed down to those who have no merit; a hand reaching down to those who have fallen into a pit. The Bible bids us believe that on the throne of the universe there is a God like that.

PRAYER

*Loving and gracious God, help me understand more
deeply than ever what it means to be a recipient of Your grace.
I have some idea, but I long to realize it even more.
Help me, my Father. In Jesus' name. Amen.*

~

FURTHER STUDY

Dan. 9:1-18; Deut. 9:5; 1 Pet. 5:5
Is grace the result of righteousness?
Who does God give grace to?

AMAZING!

*"So too, at the present time there is
a remnant chosen by grace." (11:5)*

❧

Illion T. Jones, a famous Welsh preacher, said that "the word 'grace' is unquestionably the most significant single word in the Bible." I agree. But it must be understood right away that grace is a characteristic of God which is exercised only toward those who have a special relationship with Him. Nowhere in the Bible is the grace of God mentioned in connection with humankind generally, though some theologians frequently use the term "common grace" (a term not mentioned in the Bible)—the idea that God gives a special form of grace to the whole of humankind which restrains them from being as bad as they could be.

The other day I came across a writer who said: "The creation of the universe was an exercise of grace." I understand that he might have been using the word "grace" as a synonym for love (a mistake often made by Christian writers), but strictly speaking, the exhibition of grace is reserved for the elect—those whom God foreknew would be brought into a special relationship with Him through His Son, Jesus Christ. This is why we must distinguish "grace" from "mercy" or "goodness," for Scripture says: "The Lord is good to all, And His tender mercies are over all his works" (Psa. 145:9, NKJV).

Arthur W. Pink says: "Grace is the sole source from which flows the goodwill, love, and salvation of God into His chosen people." Grace cannot be bought, earned, deserved, or merited. If it could, it would cease to be grace.

PRAYER

Father, it's truly amazing that love should stoop down to me—an undeserving, even hell-deserving sinner. Such an exhibition of grace is more than I can comprehend. But I receive it nevertheless. Because of it I am saved. Hallelujah!

≈

FURTHER STUDY

Rom. 3:1-24; Acts 15:11; 2 Tim. 2:1
What is the result of responding to God's grace?
What was Paul's exhortation to Timothy?

SOVEREIGN GRACE

FOR READING AND MEDITATION—
EPHESIANS 2:1-10

*"For it is by grace you have been saved,
through faith. . . . It is the gift of God." (2:8)*

～

In order to understand grace, we must see it in relation to a Sovereign. As one writer puts it: "Grace is bound to be sovereign since it cannot by its very nature be subject to compulsion." This is why we often refer to it as *free grace*. There is no reason for grace *but* grace.

I believe the old definition of grace cannot be improved upon: "Grace is the free unmerited favor of God." At the heart of all true communion with God, there lies this gripping truth: God took the initiative. He is more inclined toward us than we are toward Him. We cannot earn His affection. We have simply to receive it. Always the initiative is from God.

When you originally came to Him, you came because He first drew you. The very faith by which you lay hold of Him is not of yourself; it is, as our text says, "the gift of God." Every step you make on your spiritual pilgrimage is possible because of His grace.

I know this teaching affronts many modern-day men and

women, because they like to feel that they can "work their passage to heaven," as one preacher puts it. This is like someone in debt for a million pounds trying to get the one to whom he is indebted to accept his resources of a few pence as being sufficient to clear the debt. Listen to the Word of God again and let it sink deep into your soul: "For it is by grace you have been saved. . . . It is the gift of God." Grace is a gift. You have not to achieve but simply receive.

PRAYER

O Father, once again my heart is moved as I realize it was not my merit but Your mercy, acting in grace, that drew You to me, and me to you. All honor and glory be to Your mighty and everlasting name. Amen.

FURTHER STUDY

Rom. 5:1–21; Titus 3:7
How does Paul define grace?
Write out your own definition of grace.

"WE'VE WON A HOLIDAY"

"In him we have . . . the forgiveness of sins,
in accordance with the riches of God's grace." (1:7)

∼

What is it in the heart of most men and women that rejects the idea of God's free and generous offer of salvation? It is pride, the deadliest of all the deadly sins. Bernard Shaw, an example of a modern-day thinker, said: "Forgiveness is a beggar's refuge. We must pay our debts." *But we cannot pay our debts.* As our spiritual fathers saw so clearly, the only language we can use in the presence of a God who demands so much and whose demands we are unable to meet is:

Just as I am without one plea
But that Thy blood was shed for me,
And that Thou bidd'st me come to Thee,
O Lamb of God, I come, I come.

In response to our coming, the free unmerited favor of God flows down to us, cancels our debt, imputes and imparts Christ's righteousness to us. How can Christ's righteousness be imputed and imparted to us? It's *His* righteousness, not ours.

A simple illustration may help to illuminate this point. A

dull little boy came home from school one day and said to his mother: "We've won a holiday." The truth was, another boy had come top of the region in the examinations, and the head teacher decided to give the whole school a holiday. Yet the dull little lad said: "We've won a holiday."

Grace is like that. God permits the righteousness of Jesus to cover us and then—as we open ourselves to it—to enter us. He did it, but we benefit from it. Isn't grace really amazing?

PRAYER

O Father, as I contemplate still further the "riches"
of Your grace, once again I have to confess it's truly amazing.
No wonder men and women use that term to describe
Your grace. No other adjective will do! Amen.

FURTHER STUDY

Phil. 4:1-19; 1 Tim. 1:14; Titus 3:6
What has God promised?
What did Paul testify to Timothy?

The God of All Grace

"But by the grace of God I am what I am." (15:10)

Is it any wonder that throughout the history of the Christian church, men and women have found the thought of grace so overwhelmingly wonderful, they seemed unable to get over it? Grace was the constant theme of their prayers, their preaching, their writing—and their hymns. Take this for example:

> Great God of wonders, all Thy ways
> Display the attributes divine;
> But countless acts of pardoning grace
> Beyond Thine other wonders shine;
> Who is a pardoning God like Thee?
> Or who has grace so rich and free?

Many have fought to uphold the truth of God's grace, accepting ridicule and loss of privilege as the price of their stand. Paul waged war against the legalists in the Galatian churches over this matter, and the battle to uphold this great truth has gone on ever since. Augustine fought it in the fourth and fifth centuries, as did the Reformers in the sixteenth.

I sense that the church once again is in danger of losing out to legalism as more and more Christians get caught up with *doing* rather than *being*. Talk to people about what they are *doing*, and they are with you at once; talk to them about who they are *being* (who they really are), and their attitude is one of deferential blankness.

The church of Jesus Christ is in a sad state when it can't say with conviction and meaning, as did the apostle Paul: "By the grace of God I am what I am."

PRAYER

"God of all grace, give me grace to feel my need of grace. And give me grace to ask for grace. Then give me grace to receive grace. And when grace is given to me, give me grace to use that grace."
In Jesus' name I pray. Amen.

~

FURTHER STUDY

2 Cor. 1:1-12; 6:1; Gal. 2:21
Where was Paul's boast rooted?
What was Paul's warning to the Corinthians?

GOD KNOWS ALL

"I know what is going through your mind." (11:5)

~

The final aspect of God's nature that we will examine in this book is His knowledge and wisdom. I link these two characteristics together because really it is almost impossible to consider one without considering the other.

The difference between knowledge and wisdom has been described like this: "Knowledge is what we know; wisdom is the right application of what we know." God, of course, knows everything: everything possible, everything actual. He is perfectly acquainted with every detail in the life of every being in heaven, in earth, and in hell. Daniel said of Him: "He knows what lies in darkness, and light dwells with him" (Dan. 2:22). Nothing escapes His notice, nothing can be hidden from Him, and nothing can be forgotten by Him.

Many Christians, when referring to their conversion, say that God has forgotten their sins, but strictly speaking that is not so. God never forgets anything. What He promises to do with our sins is "to remember [them] no more" (Jer. 31:34). There is a great difference between forgetting something and deciding not to remember it. Realizing, then, as we do, that *God knows everything* ought to strengthen our faith and cause us to bow in adoration before Him. The hymnist put it effectively when he wrote these words:

> *The knowledge of this life is small,*
> *The eye of faith is dim,*
> *But 'tis enough that God knows all*
> *And I shall be with Him.*

PRAYER

O Father, how consoling it is to know that You know everything. Nothing ever escapes Your attention. This means I can relax, for what I don't know, You know. And because You know it, then what I don't know can't hurt me. Amen.

∾

FURTHER STUDY

Job 31:1-4; 34:21-25; Psa. 147:5
What was Job's question?
What was Elihu's response?

REFLECT ON PERFECTION

*"They will speak of the . . . splendor of your majesty,
and I will meditate on your wonderful works." (145:5)*

❧

The fact that God knows everything ought to strengthen our faith and cause us to bow down in adoration before Him. Yet how little do we reflect on this divine perfection! Those who are inclined to rebel against God hate this aspect of His being and would do away with it if they could. They wish there might be no Witness to their sin, no Searcher of their hearts, no Judge of their deeds. How very solemn are the words of the psalmist recorded in Psalm 90:8: "You have set our iniquities before you, our secret sins in the light of your presence."

To the believer, however, the truth of God's omniscience (His all-knowledge) ought to be one of tremendous comfort and security. In times of perplexity we ought to say like Job: "He knows the way that I take; when he has tested me, I shall come forth as gold" (Job 23:10). Whatever might be going on in our lives that is profoundly mysterious to us and quite incomprehensible to those who are around us, we must never lose sight of the fact that "He knows the way that [we] take."

The psalmist, when seeking to stir his soul to confidence and hope, reminded himself in the midst of his weakness and weariness: "He knows how we are formed, he remembers that we are dust" (Psa. 103:14). And Simon Peter, when his failure brought him almost to the point of despair and the searching question came "Do you love me?" said: "Lord, you know all things; you know that I love you" (John 21:17). Such knowledge should ever cause us to worship.

PRAYER

Father, help me reflect on this fact that You know everything, for I see that the more I understand it, the more secure I will feel in my soul. Teach me still more, dear Lord. In Jesus' name. Amen.

~

FURTHER STUDY

Isa. 55:1-9; Heb. 4:12-13; 1 John 3:20

What statement did God make?

What did the writer to the Hebrews confirm?

THE GOD WHO SEES

"I have now seen the One who sees me." (16:13)

~

What matters most—the fact that I know God or that God knows me? I think in a sense the latter. For my knowledge of Him depends on His sustained initiative in knowing me.

Just as the knowledge of His love for me causes the scales to fall from my eyes and turns the machinery of my soul in His direction, so my knowledge of how intimately He knows me does something similar. I am graven on the palms of His hands. I am never out of His thoughts. He knows me as a friend, and there is not a single moment when His eye is not upon me.

It was this that Hagar came to see when she was feeling utterly bereft and forgotten—that God saw her and knew everything there was to know about her. "I have now seen the One who sees me," she said. There is unspeakable comfort in knowing that God knows all about us.

Dietrich Bonhoeffer was a German pastor who was executed by the Nazis. During the days prior to his death, the thing that brought him great solace was not so much that he knew God but that God knew him. The poem he wrote in his prison cell entitled "Who Am I?" ends with the words: "Who am I? O Lord, Thou knowest I am thine." Knowing how much he was known by God brought him great comfort and consolation. He knew that whatever happened to him, it would not happen without God's knowledge.

We, too, can rest in the glorious truth that all which can be known about us is known by One who has chosen—by His own gracious will—to make Himself known to us.

PRAYER

Gracious and loving Lord, thank You for reminding me that my knowledge of You depends on Your knowledge of me. Your knowledge of me stirs my soul toward my knowing You. You initiate—I respond. Keep initiating, dear Lord. Amen.

~

FURTHER STUDY

Psa. 119:161-168; Nah. 1:7; 1 Cor. 8:3; 2 Tim. 2:19

What was the psalmist able to acknowledge?

What sort of person is known by God?

FULLNESS—ONLY IN GOD

FOR READING AND MEDITATION—
ROMANS 16:17-27

"To the only wise God be glory forever
through Jesus Christ!" (16:27)

❧

The subject of God's knowledge must be linked to His wisdom, and it is this aspect of the divine nature that we consider now. What does the Bible mean when it describes God as wise? It means the ability to use knowledge to the best possible ends. This ability is found in its fullness only in God. God is never other than wise in everything He does. Knowledge without wisdom would be pathetic, a broken reed. Wisdom without knowledge would be inoperative and quite frightening. God's boundless knowledge and wisdom are perfect in every way, and it is this that makes Him utterly worthy of our trust.

One of the great difficulties we have in the Christian life is trusting the divine wisdom. *We* can recognize wisdom only when we see the end to which it is moving. Yet God often calls us to trust Him when we can't see the end that He is pursuing. And then in such times we have to ask ourselves: "How much do I trust Him?"

Before I began speaking to a Christian youth group once, I

asked if someone could offer a definition of God's wisdom. One young man said: "God's wisdom is the ability to get us through scrapes and difficulties without getting hurt." I gave the young man full marks for attempting a definition, but I had to show him that this was not what divine wisdom is all about. The goal behind divine wisdom is not to make us happy but to make us holy. And sometimes pursuing that goal may involve us in considerable pain.

PRAYER

Father, here I am again—at the road less traveled. Help me tread the road ahead knowing that whatever pain You allow me to feel is for my good. I do not welcome it, but I do not run from it either, as long as You stay with me. Amen.

FURTHER STUDY

Psa. 104:1-24; Prov. 3:19; Rom. 11:33
Where is God's wisdom evidenced?
What was Paul's conclusion?

GOD'S ONE GREAT GOAL

*"For those God foreknew he also predestined
to be conformed to the likeness of his Son." (8:29)*

~

What is God's great goal in the universe to which His energies are devoted? We have it in our text for today. The Living Bible puts this best, and I have no hesitation in saying that although it is not regarded as a true translation (it is, rather, a paraphrase), its rendering of Romans 8:29 is one of the most exciting things I have ever read. This is what it says: "For from the very beginning God decided that those who came to him . . . should become like his Son." God's great energy and wisdom, working on behalf of all Christians, is directed to making us like His Son Jesus Christ. Of course this purpose will only be fully realized in the world to come, but while we are here, He is pursuing this selfsame purpose nevertheless.

It is only when we comprehend this that we will be able to understand the purpose that lies behind all our trials and difficulties. Romans 8:28—"And we know that all that happens to us is working for our good" (TLB)—must be read in connection with Romans 8:29. Because God is committed to making us like His Son, His wisdom goes to work on every trial that comes our way in order to bring from it something that will enrich our character and make us more like Jesus Christ.

Infinite power is ruled by infinite wisdom. He could deliver us and make our lives comfortable, but in a fallen world this is not the best purpose. Understanding this is crucial if we are to live our lives the way God desires.

PRAYER

Father, forgive me that so often my goals are diametrically opposed to Yours. Help me bring my goals in line with Your goals. I shall need Your help to adjust. Whatever happens, keep me ever moving toward becoming more and more like Jesus. Amen.

~

FURTHER STUDY

1 Cor. 1:1-31; Col. 2:3
How does Paul describe the foolishness of God?
What is hidden in Christ?

"SOME EXTRA PRACTICE"

*"Consider it pure joy, my brothers,
whenever you face trials of many kinds." (1:2)*

❧

The Bible is replete with instances of God's wisdom moving
men and women through the most difficult times to the most
wonderful ends. Take Abraham, for example. Although he is
known in Scripture as the "the friend of God," he was capable
of some shabby behavior. On one occasion he actually com-
promised his wife's chastity (Gen. 12:10-20), and later, sub-
mitting to her pressure, fathered a child by Hagar, their maid
(Gen. 16:1-16). Then, seeking to avoid Sarah's hysterical
recriminations, he allowed her to drive Hagar away from their
household (Gen. 21:8-21). Clearly, Abraham was not a man of
strong principle, and there were great flaws in his character. But
God in wisdom dealt with this man and brought him through
some great trials until he was changed from a man of the world
to a true man of God.

The same wisdom which ordered the path Abraham trod
orders our lives. We should never be taken aback when unex-
pected and upsetting things happen to us. We should recognize

that no matter how hard the trial, God's power will be there to get us through, and God's wisdom will ensure that the trial will be worth more than it costs.

I like the way Jim Packer describes what may be God's design when He permits us to go through trials: "Perhaps he means to strengthen us in patience, good humor, compassion, humility, or meekness by giving us some extra practice in exercising these graces under specially difficult situations." "Some extra practice." Some of us, myself included, sorely need it.

PRAYER

Father, help me grasp this truth once and for all, that Your wisdom ensures the trials I go through are worth far more than they cost. You are more committed to making me like Jesus than I am myself. It hurts sometimes, but deep down I am grateful.

❧

FURTHER STUDY

Isa. 48:1-10; Psa. 66:10; Mal. 3:3; 1 Pet. 1:7
What process is God's testing likened to?
What is the end result?

OUR ONLY HOPE

FOR READING AND MEDITATION—
JEREMIAH 9:17-24

*"I am the LORD, who exercises kindness,
justice and righteousness on earth." (9:24)*

❧

Let's review what we have said about God's character. We
began by recognizing that in today's church, we seem more
interested in knowing about ourselves than in knowing God.
The result of this is increased anxiety, depression, and a hundred other ills. We have also seen that God has revealed Himself
through the Scripture in many different ways: as powerful, personal, plural, having holy love, a God of wrath, trustworthy,
gracious, all-knowing, and all-wise.

It's interesting, isn't it, as our passage for today shows, that
when the Lord talks about Himself in the Scriptures, it is usually in terms of His attributes or character traits: kindness, justice, righteousness, and so on. And there is a clear and definite
purpose in this: the more we know of God, the more estab-
lished our lives will be here on the earth.

I myself am convinced that there is nothing more important
than knowing God through contemplation of Him. I am not
talking about mere intellectual knowledge. I speak of the

knowledge of God that comes through contemplation of Him, the ability to see life from His perspective, through His eyes. It means to look out at life's circumstances through the lens of faith, bearing in mind God's plan, to accept that whatever is happening is allowed by God and that everything comes under His personal surveillance. This kind of God-understanding and God-awareness is our only hope for coping with the problems of our day.

PRAYER

Father, I am convinced. I see that if I am to operate in a context of confidence, I can only do so as I look out at life through Your eyes. Help me to do more than glance at You occasionally. Help me to gaze on You continually. Amen.

FURTHER STUDY

Phil. 3:1-11; Col. 1:9-10
What was Paul's desire?
What did Paul pray for the Colossians?

TRUTH IN A NUTSHELL

FOR READING AND MEDITATION—
DANIEL 11:14-35

*"The people that do know their God
shall be strong, and do exploits."* (11:32, KJV)

～

What are the benefits of keeping our gaze continually focused on God? I can think of at least three.

First, the more we study Him, the more we will want to become like Him. The most natural thing in the world, when there is a good relationship between parents and their children, is for that child to want to become like them. That is the way it is also with God our Father. The more we discover of His love, His holiness, His purity, His trustworthiness, His strength, His patience, the more we want to emulate Him.

Second, the more we study God, the better we will know ourselves. When Isaiah stepped into the Temple and had a vision of God, he also saw the truth about himself. Things that were hidden deep within him came to light in the presence of the Eternal.

Third, the more we study Him, the clearer will be our perspective on the world. When you see that God is in charge, then you won't panic every time you open the newspaper. You can only know God, of course, through Christ, and because You have Him, instead of saying, "Look what the world has come to," you will be able to say, "Look what has come to the world."

The people who know their God will firmly resist the Adversary, says Daniel. The Amplified Bible puts it well: "The people who know their God shall prove themselves strong and shall stand firm and do exploits." I can do no more than to say—there you have it in a nutshell. The more you know God, the stronger you will be.

PRAYER

My Father and my God, now I set my course for the wide seas.
With Your truth as my compass, and Your Word as my chart,
I set sail on this great adventure, to know You better. I can count
on You, but can I count on me? With Christ's help I can. Amen.

~

FURTHER STUDY

2 Tim. 1:1-12; John 17:3; Job 19:25
What did Jesus pray?
What was the key to Job's facing his difficult circumstances?

OTHER BOOKS IN THIS SERIES

If you've enjoyed your experience with this devotional book, look for more Every Day with Jesus® titles by Selwyn Hughes.

Every Day with Jesus: The Lord's Prayer
0-8054-2735-X

Every Day with Jesus: The Spirit-Filled Life
0-8054-2736-8

Every Day with Jesus: The Character of God
0-8054-2737-6

Every Day with Jesus: Hinds' Feet, High Places
0-8054-3088-1

Available July 2004
Every Day with Jesus: The Armor of God
0-8054-3079-2

Available July 2004
Every Day with Jesus: Staying Spiritually Fresh
0-8054-3080-6

ALSO BY SELWYN HUGHES

Every Day Light   0-8054-0188-1
with paintings by Thomas Kinkade

Every Day Light: Water for the Soul   0-8054-1774-5
with paintings by Thomas Kinkade

Every Day Light: Light for the Path   0-8054-2143-2
with paintings by Larry Dyke

Every Day Light: Treasure for the Heart   0-8054-2428-8
with paintings by Larry Dyke

Every Day Light Devotional Journal   0-8054-3309-0

Christ Empowered Living   0-8054-2450-4

Cover to Cover   0-8054-2144-0
A Chronological Plan to Read the Bible in One Year

Hope Eternal   0-8054-1767-2

Jesus-The Light of the World   0-8054-2089-4
with paintings by Larry Dyke

The Selwyn Hughes Signature Series
Born to Praise   0-8054-2091-6
Discovering Life's Greatest Purpose   0-8054-2323-0
God: The Enough   0-8054-2372-9
Prayer: The Greatest Power   0-8054-2349-4

Trusted
All Over the World

Daily Devotionals

    Books and Videos

Day and Residential Courses

    Counselling Training

Biblical Study Courses

    Regional Seminars

Ministry to Women

CWR have been providing training and resources for Christians since the 1960s. From our headquarters at Waverley Abbey House we have been serving God's people with a vision to help apply God's Word to everyday life and relationships. The daily devotional *Every Day with Jesus* is read by over three-quarters of a million people in more than 150 countries, and our unique courses in biblical studies and pastoral care are respected all over the world.

For a free brochure about our seminars and courses or a catalogue of CWR resources please contact us at the following address:

CWR,
Waverley Abbey House,
Waverley Lane,
Farnham,
Surrey GU9 8EP

Telephone: 01252 784700
Email: mail@cwr.org.uk
Website: www.cwr.org.uk